HOW TO INSTALL

KODI ON FIRESTICK

Super Easy Step-By-Step Instructions (With Screenshots) to Set Up Kodi on Your Amazon Fire TV Stick in Under 10 Minutes (2020 Update)

Alexa Maxwell

Table of Contents

Introduction

How would you like to access and watch your favorite media content with your Amazon Fire TV Stick?

The Kodi Interface

I'm not just talking movies and series. But also your favorite music, games, your pictures, you name it.

Impossible?

Think again...

With *'How to Install Kodi on Firestick: Super Easy Step-By-Step Instructions (**With Screenshots**) to Set Up Kodi on Your Amazon Fire TV Stick in Under 10 Minutes'* I will show you how!

You can follow along with the instructions, and the screenshots.

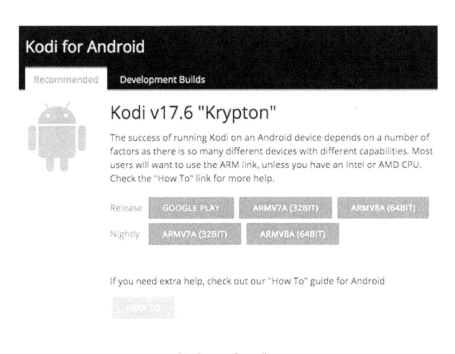

Kodi download page

All you need is an:

- Amazon Fire TV or Fire TV Stick
- Internet connection
- This book

With the Fire TV and Fire TV Stick, you have already brought an awesome mediacenter in your home. However, it does have its limitations.

If you install Kodi on your Fire TV or Fire TV Stick though, you can turn your it into **a real powerhouse**!

So, what is Kodi?

Kodi is a free open source media player. This user friendly entertainment hub brings all your digital media together in one central location.

With Kodi, you can stream all possible media content. And, this is a big one, in *any* format. I don't know about you, but this is one of my big frustrations with using a program like iTunes or Quicktime: that the player can only play certain file formats.

Not so with Kodi!

Finally, because Kodi is an open source platform, many amazing add-ons have been developed, and I will share with you my favorite ones. So, buckle up, and prepare for the media experience of a lifetime!

1. What are the Amazon Fire TV and Fire TV Stick?

You may already know what the Amazon Fire TV and Fire TV Stick are. If so, feel free to skip this chapter and continue with the next one. However, I want everybody to be on board before we get to the good stuff. So, if you don't know what the Fire TV and Fire TV Stick are, or you bought one but don't really know *what* you bought, this chapter is for you.

Don't worry, I'm not going all technical on you. You will simply learn what the Fire TV and Fire TV Stick are, what you can do with them, and how they differ. You can find all the spec details online, if you're interested.

***

Amazon Fire TV

The first generation Amazon Fire TV was launched in 2014. It is Amazon's digital media player, and comes with a microconsole remote. With the Amazon Fire TV, you can stream digital audio and video content to a high-definition television, as long as the player is connected to the internet. It is also possible to play videogames with the Fire TV. You can either use the remote that comes with it, use the mobile app, or purchase an optional game controller.

In 2015, Amazon released the second generation Fire TV. And on October 25th, 2017, the third generation was released. This newest generation of the Fire TV features:

- 4K Ultra HD and HDR support
- Dolby Atmos, which improves audio playback and video quality
- Alexa Voice Remote, allowing you to use voice control for the Fire TV

Another big change is the size: Amazon wanted to make the 3rd gen Fire TV as small as possible, and did so successfully: it nearly halved the dimensions, compared to the 2nd gen! It did mean that Amazon had to remove the ports for a microSD card reader, USB 2.0 Type-A connector and Ethernet. This makes it even more important to install Kodi, which we will get to in a bit.

With regard to wireless connectivity, nothing changed: the 3rd gen Fire TV has 802.11ac with 2×2 MIMO Wi-Fi controller, and it also supports Bluetooth 4.1.

Finally, in October 2018, Amazon released four new Fire TV Edition smart TVs.

***

Amazon Fire TV Stick

In November 2014, Amazon also released the Fire TV Stick. Unlike the Fire TV, which is a set-top box, the Fire TV Stick is, well, a plugin stick. Quite similar to how you would use a USB stick. But instead of sticking it into a

USB port on your computer, you stick it into an HDMI port on your television.

Although its hardware is slightly different, the Fire TV Stick replicates much of the functionality of the larger Fire TV. It is also bundled with a remote control. You get to choose from two variants: one with voice search, and one without.

It's cheaper than the Fire TV. At the time of writing, the Fire TV sold for $69.99 and the Fire TV Stick for $39.99.

Amazon released a new version of the Fire TV Stick late 2017, fixing all of its predecessor's problems. Mainly, it's much faster and it now also includes a voice-controlled Alexa remote. It is Kodi compatible, and you can stream content from Prime Instant Video, Netflix, Youtube, Hulu, HBO, and many more with it.

Finally, in November 2018, Amazon released the Fire TV Stick 4K.

It received raving reviews from all leading tech sites, with reviews like "*It's currently the media streaming stick to go for*" (Wired) and "*Simply the best video streamer after the Apple TV*" (What HiFi).

***

As the digital media landscape continues to evolve and customers are presented with more and more options for accessing their entertainment options, the Amazon Fire TV and Fire TV Stick definitely provide you with an easy-to-use and reasonably-priced device for enjoying your favorite content.

Now that you're up to speed with regard to what the Fire TV and Fire TV Stick are, let's look at how to install the Amazon Fire TV Stick, so that you're all set up when we're moving to the meat and potatoes of this book: installing Kodi.

2. How to Install the Amazon Fire TV Stick

Installing the Amazon Fire TV Stick is a very easy process. In just a few minutes and with only a few simple steps, you can turn your TV into a smart TV with so many functions. If you have a modern high-definition TV, then it should have an HDMI port somewhere in the back or the side. This HDMI port is where your Fire TV Stick will be installed, very similar to how you plug in a flash drive to the USB port of your PC or laptop.

The Amazon Fire TV Stick comes with a micro-USB power cable. When you first use the Fire TV Stick, you will need to plug the adapter to your wall or electric socket. Next, plug the Fire TV Stick to your TV set's HDMI port. There is an HDMI cable also included in the Fire TV Stick to extend the HDMI reach. Once it is plugged in, you can now turn on your TV set.

Using your TV's remote control, look for HDMI input, keeping in mind to use the correct HDMI port. Some TVs have multiple HDMI ports, and when you browse your TV for the Fire TV Stick installation, you may see HDMI 1, HDMI 2, or HDMI 3. Remember which HDMI port you plugged the Fire TV Stick into.

Next, the Amazon Fire TV Stick comes with a remote control as well. You will need to pair this remote control with the Fire TV Stick first before you can do anything on the Fire TV Stick itself. All you need to do is insert the batteries into the remote control, and the pairing with the Amazon Fire TV Stick should proceed automatically.

Holding the Home button down for a few seconds is another option to try if the Fire TV Stick does not respond or pair right away. If it does not, you can download the Amazon Fire app on your smartphone and go from there.

The Fire TV Stick needs a reliable WiFi connection with high-speed Internet in order to access content. Once it is plugged in, it will automatically search for available wireless networks in your house, much like any other WiFi-enabled devices. Select the WiFi network you want it to connect to and then enter the password. Once you see that it is connected, it will also begin to update or download updates and other necessary data.

The great thing about the Amazon Fire TV Stick is it automatically links to your existing Amazon account. If you do not have an Amazon account yet, it is very easy to open an Amazon account right from your Fire TV Stick, using the remote control. Once you are logged in, just go through the brief introduction of the Amazon Fire TV Stick and its features, then it will take you to the parental settings which you will need to setup.

This part of the setup process is important especially if you have younger children in the house whom you may not want accessing mature content or entertainment offerings that are not appropriate for their ages.

Setting up parental control options is a must if you just leave the Fire TV Stick plugged in to your TV set, and your children also have access to the TV set in the living room. Even If you wlll be pluggIng In the FIre TV Stlck to your bedroom TV instead, it is still a good idea to have parental control settings in place.

These are the steps you will need to take to get your Amazon Fire TV Stick installed and setup on your TV screen. Once your Fire TV Stick is installed, you can now start browsing for content using your Amazon account.

In the next chapter, we will look at Kodi, a popular app that many Amazon Fire TV (Stick) users have installed for maximum entertainment options.

3. What is Kodi?

Now we've arrived at the core of this book, the reason why you bought it: using Kodi on your Fire TV (Stick).

But what is Kodi?

***

Kodi Wasn't Always Kodi...

Kodi wasn't always named Kodi. The service has been around since 2002, but at the time it was known as the Xbox Media Center. That's right, Kodi was originally an application created for the Microsoft Xbox game console! It soon after became the Xbox Media Center. Until 2014. In that year, the XBMC Foundation, which is the power behind the scenes that operates and drives the service, renamed it once more to...Kodi.

Enough with the history lessons, on to the goodies! What can Kodi do?

***

What Can Kodi Do?

Kodi is one of the most popular media player software applications available today, and it is compatible with different platforms and operating systems. One of those being your Fire TV (Stick). It enhances your entertainment options and allow you to access more TV shows, movies, games, and other features.

Kodi is a free and open-source application, meaning it encourages developers and creators to share their own contributions. On its website, the team behind the app gives this as their inspiration and description for Kodi: "Kodi spawned from the love of media. It is an entertainment hub that brings all your digital media together into a beautiful and user friendly package. It is 100% free and open source, very customisable and runs on a wide variety of devices. It is supported by a dedicated team of volunteers and a huge community."

Because Kodi works with Windows, iOS, Android, Linux, and OSX, and has a user interface that is compatible with televisions and remote controls, it is one of the apps you would want to download to your Amazon Fire TV (Stick). Kodi supports almost all media file types today, whether these files are stored locally, on the network, or streamed via the Internet.

Music files supported by Kodi include mp3, flac, wav, and wma formats. For movie and TV lovers, the popular video formats such as mp4 and avi are supported by Kodi, and online video streaming is also available. Kodi can also be used to watch and record live TV using popular backend PVR programs such as MediaPortal, MythTV, NextPVR, or Tvheadend.

There are a number of add-ons and plug-ins you can use with Kodi to further enhance your viewing and surfing pleasure. (I will share my favorites with you later on!) Many of these add-ons were created by third-party developers, and open APIs include all sorts of media content, user interfaces, online sources, screensavers, skins and themes, visualizations, weather forecasts, and other tools you can use within Kodi.

Simply put, Kodi is your media center where you can access your movies, music, TV shows, photos, and other media content in one place. It has also become popular among homeowners as a home streaming hub where you can just connect all of your devices in the network or over the Internet. If you like to view your movies between your TV, smartphone, and tablet, for instance, Kodi allows you to seamlessly connect devices and move your content accessibility to your convenience.

***

Now, you may have a pressing question: is Kodi legal? Am I putting myself at risk by installing it?

We'll look at that next.

4. Is Kodi Legal?

Are you breaking any laws by installing Kodi? No. Let me repeat: NO!

Kodi is 100% legal. If it wasn't, your Fire TV Stick wouldn't be compatible with Kodi, would it?

However, it is a valid question to ask.

***

Kodi Controversies

Kodi has seen its share of controversies also because of some users utilize Kodi to access unauthorized or illegally-obtained content.

The open nature of the Kodi platform allows many unscrupulous individuals to develop plug-ins that allow users to illegally download or stream content.

For instance, the popularity of "fully-loaded Kodi boxes" have recently become the target of legal action because users are able to stream sports, movies, TV channels, and other content for free.

For example, in February of 2017, five people who were selling "fully-loaded Kodi boxes" were arrested in several locations across the United Kingdom. The suspects were accused of violating the copyright theft laws by selling the devices to users, with the devices themselves being modified to stream subscription content for free.

***

Kodi Is 100% Legal

It is important to understand that Kodi (the application) itself is not illegal, if you are using it responsibly. Luke Johnson, a writer for TechRadar.com, explains:

"While Kodi's name is regularly dragged up in media reports on illegally-streamed content, Kodi software itself is not illegal to use. However, the software can be utilized in such a way as to perform illegal activities, such as accessing live, copyright-protected sports broadcasts, or watching pirated copies of Hollywood films or the latest can't-miss TV series without paying."

Despite the controversy regarding Kodi, it continues to grow in popularity, and its developers have stood firm on their stand against infringing on the open-source nature of the platform. Nathan Betzen, Kodi's community and project manager, recently wrote in a blog post, stating:

"We are developers and not the police, and we have no interest in acting as police for our own software. Kodi will remain as free and as open as it always has. Feel free to continue using Kodi however you want. To us Kodi is and always will be just a tool, like a hammer, and how you choose to use that tool is up to you. We don't have any problem with users setting up their boxes however they want. We just want them to actually know what they are getting themselves into when doing so."

***

So, should you download Kodi on your Amazon Fire TV (Stick)?

Absolutely!

Just stay away from buying a fully loaded Kodi box, and focus on all the amazing stuff you can access without infringing any copyrights and you have nothing to worry about.

In the next chapter, you will learn how you can install Kodi on your Amazon Fire TV Stick.

5. How to Install Kodi on the Amazon Fire TV Stick

You're here! Let's install Kodi on your Fire TV Stick.

It is not as complicated as it may seem at first to download and install Kodi. Many Fire Stick users have preceded you, successfully. As a matter of fact, the Amazon Fire TV Stick is considered to be one of the prime (pun intended!) streaming tools for Kodi.

Just follow the easy instructions in this chapter, and in less than 10 minutes you should be able to set it all up.

These are the instructions for installing Kodi 18.4 ("Leia"), which was released in September 2019.

I will discuss two methods for installing Kodi:

- Downloader
- ES File Explorer

So, if you are somehow not able to successfully install Kodi using method 1, you should be able to set it up properly with method 2.

Before we can do so, however, you will first need to enable support for third-party apps. By default, this is switched. Understandably, because not every third-party app is reliable. However, Kodi is a highly reliable, stable application. So let's go ahead and allow support for third-party apps.

***

Enabling Third-Party Apps Support

- Turn on your fire stick.
- When you see the Home Screen, go to your Fire Stick **Settings**. You can access these by navigating to the

top, and then all the way to the right.

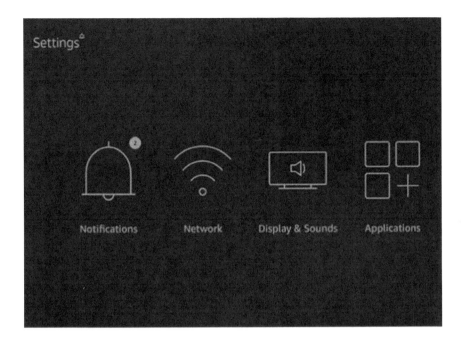

- When you are in the 'Settings' menu, scroll to the right to 'Device', and open it.

- From the list, select 'Developer Options'

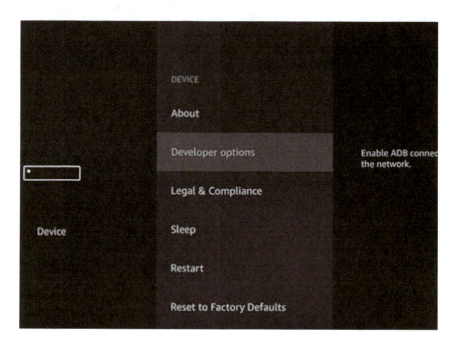

- Now, scroll down and select the option 'Apps from unknown sources'. Enable it.
- Your Fire Stick will give you a warning message, asking you if you really want to go ahead.

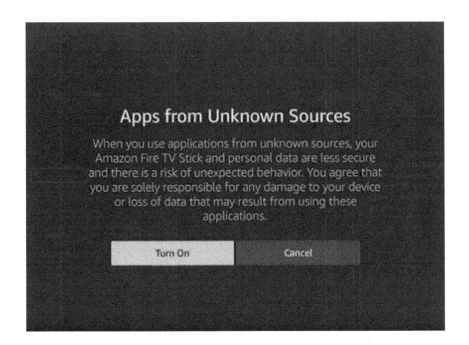

- Turn it on.

That's all there is to it. Your Fire Stick now supports third-party apps, and you are ready to install Kodi using one of the twon methods below.

***

Installing Kodi using Downloader

Of the two methods, using 'Downloader' to install Kodi is the easiest one! That's why we're starting with it.

If you somehow aren't able to install Kodi using this method, you'll have method 2 (ES File Explorer) as a backup.

- Turn on your fire stick.
- When you see the Home Screen, go to the **magnifying glass icon**. You can find it at the top left of the screen.
- Click on it.
- This is the search option on your Fire Stick. Here is where you will search for 'Downloader'.
- Type in '**Downloader**' using your virtual keyboard. As you complete typing it, you'll see the app's name appear below the virtual keyboard.

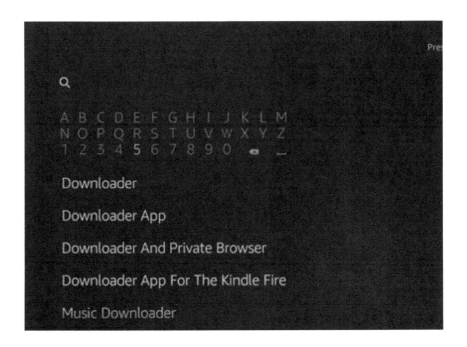

Q

A B C D E F G H I J K L M
N O P Q R S T U V W X Y Z
1 2 3 4 5 6 7 8 9 0

Downloader

Downloader App

Downloader And Private Browser

Downloader App For The Kindle Fire

Music Downloader

- Use your remote to open 'Downloader'.
- In the search results, the first one should be a large orange button with 'Downloader' on it. Select it.
- In this window, you can download and install the 'Downloader' app, which we are going to need to then install Kodi.

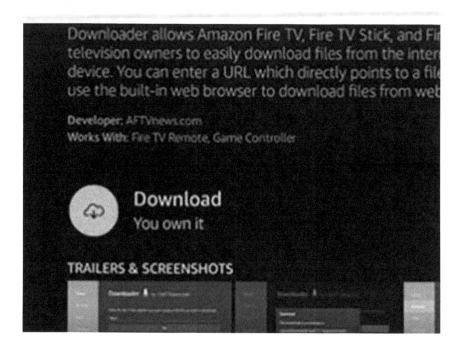

Downloader allows Amazon Fire TV, Fire TV Stick, and Fir
television owners to easily download files from the inter
device. You can enter a URL which directly points to a fil
use the built-in web browser to download files from wet

Developer: AFTVnews.com
Works With: Fire TV Remote, Game Controller

Download
You own it

TRAILERS & SCREENSHOTS

- Click on the yellow cloud icon.
- Within seconds, the 'Downloader' app will install on your Fire Stick. Once it's installed, open it.
- Ignore the welcome message, and navigate straight to '**Settings**' in the sidebar.

Home

Browser

Files

Favorites

Settings

Help

Download Folder
Folder name in /sdcard where files will be downloaded.

APK Auto-Install
Automatically ask to install APK files if downloaded.

Automatically Open Web Pages In Browser
Always open web page URLs entered on the home screen i
browser.

Enable JavaScript
Enables JavaScript in the built-in web browser.

- Here, you will want to **enable Javascript** (by default, it's disabled)
- Next, click '**Home**' in the sidebar to return to the 'Downloader' home screen
- Type in http://kodi.tv. This is Kodi's official website. When you're done, click '**Go**'.

- You are now directed to Kodi's website.

- Scroll all the way to the bottom of the page. Here, you will see an **Android logo**.

- Click on it, to go to the download section of Kodi's website.
- On the download page, scroll down until you see the **Android logo**. Click on it.

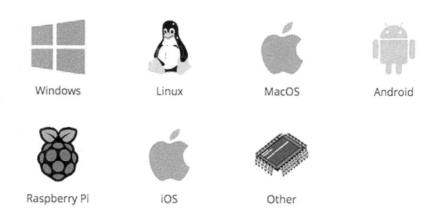

Windows   Linux   MacOS   Android

Raspberry Pi   iOS   Other

By downloading these packages or compiling from source code you agree with our general trademark policy.

- Next, find the '**ARMV7A (32BIT)**' blue button.

Kodi for Android

Recommended   **Development Builds**

Kodi v17.6 "Krypton"

The success of running Kodi on an Android device depends on a number of factors as there is so many different devices with different capabilities. Most users will want to use the ARM link, unless you have an Intel or AMD CPU. Check the "How To" link for more help.

Release   GOOGLE PLAY   ARMV7A (32BIT)   ARMV8A (64BIT)

Nightly   ARMV7A (32BIT)   ARMV8A (64BIT)

If you need extra help, check out our "How To" guide for Android

- Click this button.
- The '**Downloader**' app will now download Kodi to your Firestick. A pop-up will indicate the progress.
- When the download is complete, you will see the installation screen, with the Kodi logo in the top-left corner. At the bottom of the page, you'll see 2 buttons: '**Cancel**' 'and '**Install**'.
- Click on '**Install**'.

- Installing Kodi may take a few minutes, so this is a moment where you can make a coffee or tea in the kitchen. Almost there!
- When the installation is completed, click on '**Open**'. You will find it at the bottom-right of the page.

- Kodi will now launch on your Fire Stick.
- Again, don't be alarmed if this takes a few minutes. You can now start sipping on that coffee or tea you just made! Kodi needs a few minutes to create a database for the first time, as well as to set up everything properly. It should take this long next time

you launch Kodi.

That's it, you have no installed Kodi. In less than 10 minutes! Time to explore Kodi!

Yet...this is technology. Something always goes wrong. For some. Maybe it's you. I'm truly sorry to hear that.

But don't worry!

I hear you. And I anticipated this might happen.

Therefore, I included a 2nd, alternative method to install Kodi. Using ES File Explorer.

***

Installing Kodi using ES File Explorer

Of the two methods, using 'ES File Explorer' is a little bit more complicated than using 'Downloader'. That's why we started with 'Downloader'. Why take the long route if we can also take the shortcut, right?

But if you weren't successful using the first method, let's try the 'ES File Explorer' to install Kodi.

Reminder: make sure you enabled Third-Party Apps Support. See the instructions at the beginning of this chapter.

- We're starting the same way as with method 1: Turn on your fire stick.
- When you see the Home Screen, go to the **magnifying glass icon**. You can find it at the top left of the screen.
- Click on it.
- This is the search option on your Fire Stick. Here is where you will search for '**ES File Explorer**'.
- Type in '**ES File Explorer**' using your virtual keyboard. As you complete typing it, you'll see a list of search results appear below the virtual keyboard. *Note: you can also use Alexa voice remote.*

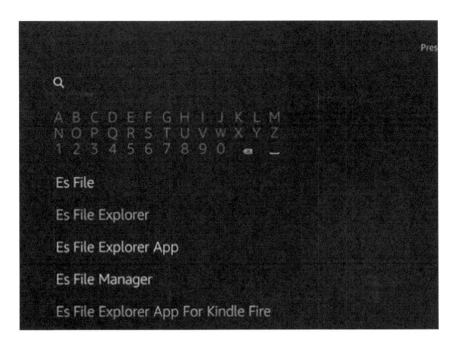

Es File

Es File Explorer

Es File Explorer App

Es File Manager

Es File Explorer App For Kindle Fire

• Select '**ES File Explorer**' from this list

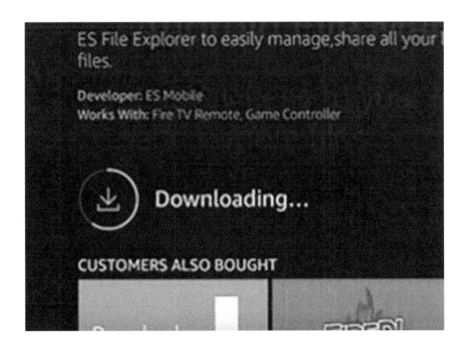

ES File Explorer to easily manage, share all your files.

Developer: ES Mobile
Works With: Fire TV Remote, Game Controller

Downloading...

CUSTOMERS ALSO BOUGHT

- Next, download and install 'ES File Explorer'.
- After the app has been installed successfully, open it.
- When you've opened the 'ES File Explorer' app, navigate to '**Favorites**' in the left sidebar.
- Next, click on '**Add**'

- Now, you'll need to fill in 2 fields:
  - 'Path'
  - 'Name'
- In the '**Path**' field, fill in this exact URL: **bit.ly/ firestickkodi2020**. This is a shortened link to download the latest Kodi version: 17.6.

- It doesn't really matter what you fill in in the '**Name**' field. It can be Kodi, or anything else. This is the name you'll be able to find Kodi under in your favorites. For this example, I'll use Kodi as a name.
- Go back to the left sidebar, and go to Favorites.

- Here, select '**Kodi**' (or if you chose a different name, choose that name)
- Once you click on it, ES File Explorer will open a new web page and you'll see a notification that the download has started.

- Return to the left side bar. Scroll all the way down. Then go all the way to the right.
- Click on the '**More**' button. You'll find it at the bottom-right.
- In the pop-up window, select '**Open in Browser**'.

- You'll probably see multiple options under '**Open With**'. Select '**ES Downloader**' and click on '**OK**'

Download sta

Open with

 ES Downloader

 com.amazon.tv.intentsupport.TvIntentSupport..

- The Kodi file should now start downloading.
- When the download is complete, click '**Open File**'.
- Next, click '**Install**'.
- You should now see the Kodi installation screen.
- Click on '**Install**'. Like with method 1, this may take a few minutes.

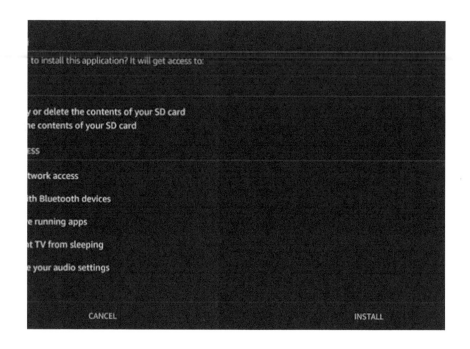

to install this application? It will get access to:

y or delete the contents of your SD card
he contents of your SD card

ESS

twork access

th Bluetooth devices

e running apps

t TV from sleeping

e your audio settings

CANCEL   INSTALL

- After the installation is complete, click on '**Open**' to launch Kodi.

That's how you use ES File Explorer to install Kodi! You can now find Kodi by navigating to the installed apps on your Fire TV Stick.

***

Installing Kodi is only the beginning. The fun really begins when you start installing Kodi add-ons. In the next chapter, I will share with you my ten favorite Kodi apps!

6. How To Install Kodi Add-Ons

If you remember, Kodi is an open source entertainment hub. This means that any party can use the Kodi source code to develop amazing add-ons and make them available for Kodi users. Like yourself!

To really take advantage of the powerhouse that Kodi is, you will want to download and install add-ons. You will need these to stream media content from the web. With those, and without spending a lot of your hard-earned cash, Kodi will soon become your one-stop shop entertainment hub.

A good place to start looking for add-ons is the Official Kodi Repository. You can also download apps you can't find here from Third Party Repositories, but I suggest you start simple.

Here's how you can access the Offical Kodi Repository:

- In the main menu, navigate to '**Add-ons**'.
- Click on 'Install from repository'
- Then, select 'Kodi Add-on repository'
- Here you can browse by category.
- Pick the add-on you like!

***

That is how you install add-ons using the Official Kodi Repository.

Next up, I will share with you my ten favorite Kodi apps!

7. Ten Must-Have Kodi Add-Ons

To get you on your way, in this chapter I will share with you my ten must-have Kodi add-ons.

Note: Every now and then, some popular Kodi add-ons are shut down because they were targeted by Internet Service Providers (ISPs). I do my best to keep this book as up to date as possible, but there is a chance that one of the add-ons below just got shut down when you are trying to install it. If that happens, don't worry: there will be other add-ons available that offer the same functionalities.

So, without further ado, let's get to it!

***

VPN Add-Ons

1. EXPESSVPN

Although it is not necessary to have when running Kodi, I still highly recommend you use a VPN. One thing you will want to keep in mind is that some of the third-party add-ons may stream content for which they do not have the proper license. There are some stories of users receiving a copyright infringement notice. With a VPN, you are not only able to surf anomously.

My advice to you is: **better safe than sorry**. If you are going to use these add-ons, make sure you use a VPN. VPN stands for Virtual Private Network, and basically allows you to browse anonymously, through a secure and private tunnel between two devices.

It can also help in unblocking content that is only available in certain geographical locations. This is very handy, as there are quite a few Kodi Add-Ons that have these geographical restrictions (meaning: you can only access them from certain parts of the world). With ExpressVPN, you can circumvent that.

There are other VPN add-ons. However, ExpressVPN is considered the top-rated Kodi VPN add-on at the moment.

***

Video Add-Ons

2. COVENANT

Covenant is one of the best and most popular video add-ons. It is considered a replacement for Exodus, which – until July 2017 – was one of the best video add-ons.

It was briefly abandoned by its developer. However, a new version was released not much later. Covenant is one of the best add-ons if you like movies and TV series. On top of that, it is very easy to navigate.

3. INCURSION

Incursion is another very popular add-on for Kodi. It's nearly identical to Exodus, which was a very popular add-on before it was shut down. It has a wide variety of streaming capabilities. Not just movies, but also TV shows! Really one of best add-ons to get started with.

4. FILM-ON SIMPLE

Are you into educational movies? Then you should definitely check out FilmON. FilmON is an online repository of educational films and documentaries. Divided in different niche categories, you'll be able to easily navigate to the type of content you want to watch.

5. USTVNOW

USTVNOW has been around on Kodi for a while. With this add-on, you can watch numerous live American channels. Especially handy for Americans not living in the U.S.

Sports Add-Ons

6. FOX SPORTS GO

Whether you're into watching live sports or on-demand content, Fox Sports is one of world's leading sports streaming services. It's an official Kodi add-on. However, if you're based outside of the US, you may need to use a VPN (such as ExpressVPN) to watch Fox Sports Go.

Install Fox Sports Go and you'll have many nights of watching your favorite sports ahead of you!

7. RED BULL TV

You've probably seen one or two Red Bull TV videos. Perhaps it was Felix Baumgartner record-breaking skydive from space, or one of Red Bull's many extreme sports videos. You can now also watch their content with Kodi.

Red Bull TV is an official Kodi add-on. If you are into adrenaline-filled sports, you'll definitely want to give this one a try.

8. PLANET MMA

I'm a massive MMA fan. If you are like me, watching the UFC events religiously, this is the #1 add-on you should install.

This add-on has lots of amazing UFC and Mixed Martial Arts content. On top of that, you'll also find live programming and on-demand videos. So, definitely one of the first add-ons you should check out!

***

Cartoon Add-Ons

9. INCURSION

Incursion is another popular Kodi add-on. It offers a wide variety of entertainment, organized in a way that allows for easy navigation between the different menus. It stands out because of its anime TV content.

10. SOUTH PARK

"You will respect my authoritah!" Who doesn't love Eric Cartman and his friends?

With over 20 seasons, this is one of the longest running animated TV-shows ever. And with this add-on, you'll have all episodes in one place. Did anyone say binge-watch?

***

There are countless Kodi add-ons. With my ten personal favorites, I'm only scratching the surface. I very much encourage you to do your own research. Explore. And find the ones you like best!

Final Thoughts

There you have it: you have been initiated into the Kodi universe!

Let's recap what you have learned. You now know:

- The difference between the Amazon Fire TV and Fire TV Stick
- How to install the Amazon Fire TV Stick
- What Kodi is
- That Kodi is 100% legal
- How to install Kodi on the Fire TV Stick
- Ten must-have Kodi add-ons to start your journey

I encourage you to now continue on your own. Have you ever seen a little kid on its bicycle, supported by the loving arm of its parent on its back, cycling next to him? And then...a push...and it's cycling without any support!

Perhaps this is how you taught your own kid to ride a bike.

As we come to the end of this book, I'm giving you that last push...

I wish you all the best, and lots of viewing pleasure, as you explore what Kodi has to offer.

The future is here. Be a part of it!

Alexa Maxwell

www.ingramcontent.com/pod-product-compliance
Lightning Source LLC
La Vergne TN
LVHW052314060326
832902LV00021B/3893